ALTHEA RE-B

"the emotional challenges one survivor faces after chemo for Ovarian Cancer"

ANNETTE BENNINGTON MCELHINEY
(Diagnosed with Ovarian Cancer III C 07/08)

Copyright © 2012 Dr. Annette Bennington McElhiney
All rights reserved.
ISBN: 1479132993
ISBN 13: 9781479132997

Yes I know.

You are asking yourself " Why am I reading a booklet entitled 'Althea Rebalances her Life' with a ditzy tight rope walker on the front cover. This cover picture seems totally unrelated to Ovarian Cancer!" When I picked up my brush, painted, and saw this image emerge, I asked myself nearly the same question. Where has this "bimbo"in teal come from?

Well let me explain by telling you my story. After being diagnosed with Ovarian Cancer IIIC in 07/08, I had to remake myself somehow. As a young girl, I grew up on a farm in Missouri with parents who were not educated. Because we had little money, I went to a Lutheran nursing school and got an RN diploma. Yet I wanted a college education, so after marrying my high school sweetheart, I went back to school as a young mother, and got several degrees in English. After that, I began teaching English literature and Women's Studies in college and continued with that off and on for 20 years. When I was diagnosed with Ovarian Cancer in 08, I'd been retired for 6 years. After the diagnosis, any confidence I had built up in myself through education and experience was totally destroyed. Yet I knew I had to rebuild my life and remake myself.

I felt there were two women warring within me. On the one hand, my former left brain nurse/teacher self told me to "keep my chin up," "be brave," "don't complain," "follow Dr's. orders," and "make plans for a short life with Ovarian Cancer." On the other side, my right brain creative self raged, wailed, defied everyone, wanted to slap people who complained about common ailments like a cold, or sunburn and who, without knowing anything about Ovarian Cancer, said "you are going to be jusssst fine!"

I struggled during chemo with the physical aspects of coping with the disease. After chemo, other, perhaps, even more disturbing emotional issues like this split personality arose. Somehow I had to merge the two, and, eventually, Althea was born when she surfaced for me in my paintings. I am not a professional painter as I had never painted before I retired from teaching in college 8 years ago; I'd always wanted to paint but lacked the confidence to put brush to canvas because I knew I'd never be a "really good painter." Therefore, I thought "Why try?" But something or someone (maybe a sleeping Althea within me who was afraid of nothing) provoked me to try. I am certainly glad I took this risk as painting has been a lifesaver for me during recovery. Soon I discovered that my chosen medium was acrylic and my emphasis was on bright colors, thick paint, texture and use of mixed media like yarn, sequins, twigs, feathers and fabric. I liked to touch the paintings and feel something sensual rather than simply a flat surface. I always liked purple and lavender (representing gynecological cancers, I'm told), but I found myself after chemo drawn to teals, greens and blues for my pallet. Painting took me into a completely different world than the left brain world I'd always lived in as a nurse and teacher - a world in which I was free to experiment and see what surfaced. I could paint for 8 hours without eating or drinking and be totally absorbed.

After I was first diagnosed and went through 5 grueling months of paclitaxal/carboplatin/bevacizamab (+ an additional 12 months maintenance of "bev" as suggested in the GOG 218 protocol) I was too fatigued and "brain fogged" to paint. During that time, I reverted to my earlier mode of expression which was writing (after all in my other left brain life I was an English literature teacher) and wrote a Memoir entitled "Where I Go When I am Silent: my first six months after being diagnosed with OC III C." In this rather self-pitying piece, I dwelt on my fears, rage, grief, isolation, and jealousies; it was a piece I wasn't proud of and shared with only a few people; however, it was honest and helped me process my initial feelings. I had written it in response to my husband's question "Why do you go silent when a commercial comes on celebrating a 60th wedding anniversary or a woman's 90th birthday?" Of course I went silent because I doubted I would ever have either as I'd been told immediately after surgery "You have a 25-30 per cent chance of living 5 years." I was devastated and completely beaten down. I didn't have the energy to read, watch TV or even eat. The few times I tried to paint, the paintings were so dark and bleak, they depressed even me! The left brain part of me didn't want to tell people I was depressed because they would think I was weak and my family and friends would worry as well.

Recovering from chemo was very slow and I wrestled with life for the next year trying to develop a plan for coping with this devastating disease. Because my husband and I had been living 6 months in California and 6 months in Colorado, I had surgery in Colorado and a great oncologist/

internist in California but had to search for a new gynecological oncologist. My first try wasn't successful. I sought a consultation with a nationally known gyn/onc who gave me a similarly bleak prognosis. He said "it really doesn't matter what you do, you will eventually die from Ovarian Cancer anyway." I was as crushed as I had been at my diagnosis immediately after surgery. However, the right brain side of me – that side which has spunk or the Althea side - began to emerge and my paint brush saved me. I was down in the dumps for a week until one day when I was painting, my brush seemed to be operated by someone other than me. The ugliest man with horns and fire licking his cheeks appeared on my canvas. I keep that painting in my garage just to remind me "I'll show that Dr. he is wrong." I am hoping that I will live many years and I'll die of a heart attack; I'd like for my family to send the painting to him then with a little note I'll have pasted on the back telling him what such a negative prognosis did to me, and does to others, at least for awhile.

Renewed and feeling more courageous after expressing my anger, I continued my search until I found a wonderful woman Dr. and her gynecological nurse assistant at Cedars Sinai, who, on the first visit, both gave me big hugs. After examining me and reviewing my medical records, she said "My job is to keep you alive for the next 10 years and by that time there will be a cure." My Dr's, and her oncological nurse's, caring attitude and encouragement were just what I needed. That statement changed my attitude and my life. From that time forward, that part of me who is Althea took over and I regained some control over my life. Some day I'm certain that Althea will pop up on my canvas ranting against doctors who only focus on statistics when each patient is really "her own statistic," but that painting probably won't emerge until, or if, I've survived past the magic 5 year mark.

After having this Dr. on my side, I could make plans for regaining my confidence and my life. Emotionally, I knew I needed the constant presence of two things, amongst many others, if I were to survive and live: love and hope. While I was in chemo, I missed my 23 year old cat who sat on my lap and purred. We had to put her to sleep because of a health problem, 6 years earlier. So I adopted 2 Bengal kittens and named them Liebe (Love in German and the middle name of my German grandmother – Matie Fredericka Liebe Carolina Block Eilers) and Hoffie (short for Hoffnung which is German for hope). They seem to know when I need their love. The two of them sit not more than 5 feet from me whenever I either paint or write. Sometimes, Hoffie (the spunky "Althea-like" one) even jumps up on my lap and prances on the computer keyboard. The unconditional love they give me and the hope they inspire in me help me keep my balance every day.

In addition, I stopped painting pictures that were purely representational and began painting pictures that revealed my deepest feelings. Before cancer, I'd often painted pregnant women or women and children. Consequently, it was no surprise to me that all my paintings after diagnosis had a woman only as a central figure and one who always had some of the same characteristics. As a child and adult, things I'd always liked about myself were my hair, my hands and my feet. My hair was always shiny and healthy so having a "bad hair day" everyday as a bald woman during chemo was a real downer for me. My body has always been large, but my hands and feet were both small and I liked that. After chemo, I began to notice that not only did the women flowing from my brush emerge either hairless or with their heads covered, but they also had no faces, no hands or no feet. It took me awhile to realize that just as Althea surfaced, some of my buried feelings were appearing. When I was in chemo, I always felt as if instead of having a distinct face, I had a big OC stamped on my forehead and was primarily known as the woman with Ovarian Cancer. In addition, after chemo I had fairly severe neuropathy in my feet and some in my hands, neuropathy which has still not gone away. Consequently, subconsciously I was always aware of my lack of hair, my numb feet and my cramped hands. So the I/ Althea in the paintings that emerged never had a face, her hair was either inappropriate colors or covered with feathers, and her hands and feet always seemed to disappear into the paintings' background.

As I continued recovering, I realized I wanted out of the hole I'd dug for myself by cutting myself off from others, by painting nondescript things and by going silent. I decided to become, once again as I was prior to my diagnosis, an "up front" and "just watch me do it" kind of woman. My husband had to call my bluff once before when I was a new mother pursuing a bachelor's degree in college. When everything seemed insurmountable to me in balancing classes and our newly born son, he said "If you can't stand the heat, get out of the kitchen." Even though he knew that taunt would "tick me off," he also knew it would prod me to redouble my efforts and get a degree. It worked and I did!

Remembering who I'd been prior to diagnosis crept into my painting and Althea was born. She became dominant and visible for all to see. I chose the name Althea for the central figure in my paintings because the word comes from the Greek word "self-healer." I knew that if I were to live and enjoy life, I had to meet my life as it is now on my own terms - Althea's terms also- with courage, determination and verve. Because my Memoir somehow seemed maudlin, in letting Althea's point of view emerge, I could see the humor in my over reactions to so many things we face all our lives in having Ovarian Cancer.

The title "Althea Re-balances her Life" and the painting on the cover illustrate exactly what I'm doing every day in balancing enjoyment of no evidence of cancer and hope against reality, grief and fears of its return. When I was a little girl growing up on a farm in Missouri, I spent hours walking the top rail of the white wooden fence that surrounded the cattle lot. I used a bamboo fishing pole to keep my balance and pretended I was in the circus. I always tried to fall on the lawn side rather than the lot side as the lot side smelled! Because I believe every experience we have in life is a learning experience, that activity must have both prepared me for my life now (which is a circus of sorts and definitely a balancing act) and been the seed for this painting of Althea balancing on the tight rope.

I am not writing this booklet and including these paintings because I think I'm special or because I have all the answers. Instead I'm letting my Althea side emerge in all her crazy ways to share how I felt and feel. I can always hear her saying in my ear, "I have the disease and I might as well learn to live with it and hope for the best." Picturing her in some of these predicaments allows me to see that perhaps I take myself too seriously, focus too much on the unpleasant things, and don't enjoy life in the here and now. In other words, I'm not doing a very good job of the balancing on the tight rope act.

Let's face it. You who have Ovarian Cancer, as well as I, are all members of a club that none of us wanted to join: the Cancer Club or CC for short. Consequently, this booklet is written for us! Outsiders often won't "get the paintings," but I'm hoping you will and that each will bring a laugh or at least a smile to your face.

Also, perhaps a more practical reason for writing this booklet is because before I had chemo, I was given lots of reading material on Ovarian Cancer, its staging, chemo's side effects, and hints for coping with the side effects etc. However, not much was said about what happens emotionally after you complete chemo, and I was too chemo-foggy to ask. When I completed my 4 initial chemo infusions and changed locations for the rest, I was given a bouquet of flowers marking my graduation and was told to go off and live my life. Just as mother never told me what marriage and motherhood would be like (been married to my high school sweetheart for 48 years, have 2 sons, and 3 grandchildren) no one ever told me that just when you complete chemo and begin to live your life, all kinds of emotional surprises ambush you. These paintings are visual images of my experiences with each wait, bump, report etc. I'm hoping as you look at these pictures, you will say "By golly I think she got it."

So please bear with me as Althea my second self/I, share my experiences after I completed my 8 rounds of taxi/carob/bev.

Like most of you, my initial diagnosis took me by surprise, even if I had gone to a diploma nursing school before college and had practiced one year as an RN. Also, even though, as a young woman I'd had what the Dr's. in the 60's called a spastic colon and endometriosis, after menopause, my bowel problem was no worse or no better and, of course, my endometriosis seemed to regress. At age 67, I had none of the warning signs of Ovarian Cancer: frequency of urination, bloating, feelings of being full after eating or other listed symptoms. Instead, I had 2 tiny spots of post menopausal bleeding spread over a month. I thought at that time that I might have uterine cancer but didn't suspect ovarian. I called my ob/gyn and was scheduled immediately for a vaginal sonogram. As I watched the pictures on the screen, saw a large black sheet covering the uterus, and watched the technician's face, I knew I was in deep trouble. A CT scan the next day confirmed the sonogram's suggested diagnosis. My CA 125 was only 47. Within a week of diagnosis, I had surgery, a diagnosis of Ovarian Cancer IIIC and a prognosis of 25-30% chance of living 5 years.

It took me awhile to process that information and for my old confidence (the Althea side of me) to kick in. I also had to remember my husband's taunt 44 year ago "if you can't stand the heat, get out of the kitchen." Consequently, I went back to my surgeon/doctor and said. "I've never ever been in the bottom third or quarter of my class and I don't intend to be in those categories in this DISEASE either." Of course, underneath, I was really scared out of my mind, but that bravado somehow helped me through the chemo. For that, and perhaps my insistence on having bevacizamab along with the more traditional pacilitaxol/carboplatin, I received the nickname "trouble." Each time I'd go in for chemo, he'd say "Here comes trouble." In some ways, that name only galvanized my determination to fight the disease with everything I had.

Like most of you, my experience with chemo wasn't pleasant. I was very anemic and also fatigued. I had after each infusion, the "cement leg syndrome" where one minute I would be fine and the next minute I'd feel as if I were walking in cement. One of these days, I'll bet I'll be painting and Althea will emerge with cement buckets on her feet, but for now I'm trying to forget those days during chemo and focus on living each day fully present and enjoying each aspect.

ALTHEA AWAITS THE RESULTS OF HER FIRST CT/PET SCAN©

After completing chemo, I had my first CT scan. The anxiety of waiting for the results was horrible. My first post surgery/chemo CT report initially said there were some suspicious shadows and the radiologist recommended a PET. I had the PET several days before Christmas and had to wait yet several more days for the report. That Christmas was truly the worst I've had in my life as I was certain the shadows meant the cancer had not been killed by the chemo. Consequently, I asked for, and received 2 more chemo infusions. Thankfully, the PET report showed "no hot spots" and my organs were "unremarkable." That was the only time in my life "being unremarkable!" was a positive characteristic.

Yet that wait, and the wait for the results of the 3 CT/PET's I have had since, always provokes deep anxiety in me. The painting of Althea on the see saw opposite NED (no evidence of disease) is a humorous expression of my feelings that first time. I've always been an obsessive researcher and reader. I also have a son who is an oncology business manager who advised me on the newest treatment and also on what is going on in clinical trials for the pharmacetutical treatment of Ovarian Cancer. Therefore, I knew that after chemo, the distinct possibility of still having measurable tumor left, of having a partial response, of having stable disease or of having a complete response to the chemo existed. The coveted response, naturally, was complete response to chemo or NED So every time I waited, I felt my fate was in the balance.

Also for the first 3 CT/PET scans, when friends or family suggested making holiday or vacation plans I always answered "let's wait until the results of my CT/PET scan" before making any plans. Only now, 2 years after surgery, am I finally realizing those 3 weeks or so aren't going to make lots of difference anyway so I might as well make the plans. Not only must I/Althea walk a tight rope, but I have to balance and weigh my chances of another NED report or "hot spots seen" each time. Different Dr's. seem to have different regimens of doing these scans. I've had one every 6 months and now at 2 years, if my CA125 and HE4 (more about both later) stay down, I will go to one a year. Yet I know I "will be on pins and needles" every time I wait for a report.

ALTHEA DANCES WITH NED©

    Fortunately, my first and all CT/PET scans since Dec. 08 have come back NED. Like the sassy Althea, I've tried throughout to keep a "stiff upper lip" and not cry or whine about my illness or the difficulty of waiting for results. But upon hearing NED, I always burst into tears because it feels like a reprieve from an immediate prison sentence. Being a former nurse, I realize intellectually that even if there is residual disease, that is not a death sentence, but in my heart, I'm still terrified. Like Althea, the tootsie-on- the-tightrope, each time I wait for a report, I feel as if the rope is in a brisk wind and I'm barely staying on it. The relief of letting myself drop off momentarily and cry is profound. However, the relief lasts only until it is time for the next scan.

    Also, I find myself politely, not in outrageous Althea style, explaining to folks not in the CC:

    "No! Having no evidence of disease does not mean I'm cured." Althea would say:

    "You idiot – a cure in Ovarian Cancer only comes when you've been NED 5 years or more. And even then, you aren't really cured because it could return in year 6 or year 10. Can't you just let me enjoy the present reprieve and not remind me that I'm still in danger?" But I often try, in left brain style, to educate them without alienating them. However, I think a future painting will probably be one of Althea biting her own tongue to keep from coming unglued when people ask these questions or others like them.

Also many people would tell me when I wore my wig "I can tell you are all over the cancer because you look so good and your hair looks so real." They had no idea what an issue "not having hair" can be for women – especially those like me who considered it my best asset. That was difficult! I would get up in the morning and look in the mirror. I would see an Althea that only my parents saw – one with no hair or as bald as the bare butt of a baby. When I caught a glimpse of myself in the mirror, I felt naked and very vulnerable. So if I needed to feel like my familiar self, I would wear one of the wigs I have.

Yet I'm rather ashamed to say, as Althea I felt a certain power in shocking people. For example, I wore a wig to the office of my cardiologist. As he entered the examining room, I said, I'm trying to decide if I should shock you or not. He, not knowing I'd had chemo or Ovarian Cancer, said "shock me." I whipped off my wig and the poor man turned white and kept patting me on the shoulder. I realized that perhaps my desire to be "shocking" was really a rather cruel thing to do. But doing so, somehow, made me laugh and feel like I wasn't a total victim. I was still Althea, the courageous, outrageous and feisty one who wasn't letting cancer get her down.

While chemo and cancer could devastate my body, it could not completely stifle my/Althea's spirit. Althea's chosen hair style in each of these paintings illustrates the state of her spirit.

ALTHEA FINDS NICKI'S CIRCLE

    One of the most difficult aspects of having Ovarian Cancer for me has been the loneliness. Because I live one half a year in one state and the other half in another, I have 2 very different sets of friends.

    When I was in a crowd with healthy women my age or older, all laughing, dancing, or eating, I would feel like "the odd one out." Frequently, I would go silent but still be thinking and feeling. My world as a cancer survivor was entirely different from theirs. They were worrying about their next hair appointment and I was worried about having hair or the possibility of losing it again if I had a reoccurrence. They were complaining about their next year's plans and I was wondering if I would even be here next year. But before becoming Althea, I kept quiet and "just felt different and very alone." Even my spouse of 48 years sometimes couldn't reach me. I didn't want him to know how depressed and scared I was because I knew that would affect him.

    In addition, nearly everyone I met knew someone who had breast cancer, but very few knew about the silent killer Ovarian Cancer. Many women I met also were long time survivors of breast cancer. They would say you are going to be jussst fine! I'd nod and say I hope So, but again feel that profound loneliness because the disease I had was far more lethal than breast cancer is. Before seeking a support group, I knew no one who had Ovarian Cancer or with whom I could identify.

Having a support group of others like you helps much in keeping your feelings of hope and, yet, your fears in balance. The one place I feel I can "completely let go" and share how I feel is at the support group I found in Colorado, Nicki's Circle, sponsored by the Colorado Ovarian Cancer Alliance. Sometimes 30-40 women attend, in all stages of survivorship: some before their surgery, some during chemo, and some who are long time survivors. At each session, everyone has an opportunity to speak or ask questions related to their concerns at that particularly point in time.

Unlike in the crowd of "outsiders," here I felt embraced and welcomed. I watch as women break down and others in the group come forward to pat their hands, hand them a Kleenex or just give them their silent respect. These meetings serve to replenish my reserve of strength so that I can go on to face whatever I must in the next month.

In part, I am trying to create with the humorous Althea painting series that same sense of identification or recognition of how each of us feels as we fight our respect battles against the disease. Alone I sometimes feel as if I am going bananas, but the women in this group let me know that they experience the same "ups and downs" that I do. I'm hoping these paintings will be visual reminders to you, as well as to me, of the same.

The role that maintenance drugs may or not play in Ovarian Cancer is debatable and the actual data supporting the good and the bad are unreliable. Today, as for many years, women with Ovarian Cancer generally have 6-8 rounds or pacilitaxol/carboplatin every 3 weeks and then everyone watches and waits to see if the cancer will return. Currently, clinical studies are in process on different delivery methods. Sometimes they give chemo 3 weeks on and then 1 week off. In addition, sometimes they pair the pacilitaxol/carboplatin with various targeted drugs. Some women even have pacilitaxol weekly after completing their initial therapy.

Because I had bevacizamab for one year after the initial 8 chemos, I didn't experience the "cutting loose" phase of Ovarian Cancer treatment until I was out nearly 18 months. During that time, I felt as if I was at least partially protected as the biological drug was cutting off blood supply to any "lurking cancer" cells left behind after the initial therapy. During that time, I also had the care and support from oncologists and oncology nurse specialists to buoy me up and give me a sense of security.

ALTHEA FLIES WITHOUT A NET©

Then it stopped! Suddenly, I was finished! Then the reality of having had Ovarian Cancer really hit me! One day I was driving and I saw a poster advertising an arts festival. On it was an "Althea like" character who was joyfully swinging on her trapeze. As I looked at the poster on the pole, I thought, I feel like I'm on a trapeze but I am flying without a net and I could crash to the ground at any second. I no longer have the medical support but am totally dependent on my body, my brain and my spirit to deliver. I went home, and guess what? On the canvas Althea emerged again, hanging, not joyfully, but precariously with nothing beneath her but her hope that something would save her, professional caretakers, her body or her determined spirit.

Yes, I know: Althea is always either teetering on a tight rope, balancing on a see saw, hanging from a trapeze, or now hanging from her hands from a tree. Yet it seems to me that one of the things ovarian survivors must do lots of is wait suspended: wait for CA 125 reports, wait for CT/PET scans and wait to see if the dreaded cancer returns. Sometimes all the waiting gets to me and I feel very discouraged.

ALTHEA AWAITS HER CA 125 REPORT©

Even though I was a practicing nurse years ago, I don't remember much about CA 125. Now it sometimes seems that "my numbers" rule my emotions or my sense of security. Those of us with Ovarian Cancer share, I think, the same concern for our CA 125 report. If the number goes up, we worry, and if it goes down, we take a deep sigh of relief.

Today a controversy rages about how much emphasis should be put on a rising CA 125 if the survivor has no symptoms. Should one take chemo as soon as the CA 125 shows a pattern of rising or should one wait until symptoms occur or something appears on a CT/ PET scan? Some Dr's. say one and some say the other. Some say they know that having frequent CA 125 tests causes unnecessary anxiety in survivors, but still continue to order them. For me, like with the CT/ PET scans, I usually feel enormous relief if the number stays the same.

Yet I don't know if the CA 125 is a good marker for me because I haven't had a reoccurrence which the number predicted. My pre surgery CA 125 was only 47, after surgery it jumped to 75 (due to inflammation), after first chemo to 12, and then down to 6. My recent CA 125 test results have fallen between 1-6. Consequently, my Dr. has added the HE4 test as well. Normal limits on that test are anything below 150. I've had three test results thus far: 107, 70, and 77. I want to believe that if the one test doesn't catch a return of cancer, the other one will. But who knows? So is it any wonder that Althea feels she is hanging on by her fingertips (except of course we can't see them as she can't feel her fingers either).

Also, just as a single woman dominates this Althea series, the numbers between 1-6 and 70-107 show up in many of my paintings. I realize that I'm slightly obsessed with them, but can't seem to stop. I don't even sleep well for about a week before my results appear. When non club members look at my paintings they say: "So what is it about these numbers? They appear again, and again, and again. Why are they important?" Of course Althea would say "Duh. Don't you get it – those are my CA 125 numbers." But once again, I restrain myself, refrain from her retort and simply try to explain that they can indicate a reoccurrence and, therefore, they are important

ALTHEA REACTS TO A BAD REPORT©

Last summer of 09, my number jumped from 3 to 6 in one three week period and I was an emotional disaster. I was certain, especially because my number had doubled in three weeks that the ugly beast was returning! Immediately I was on the internet looking up other possible reasons for a jump like that. The oncology nurses tried to reassure me that the bad sinus infection I had (gave me heavy duty antibiotics for that) had driven my number up. But the wait from that "bad for me" report until the next one 3 weeks later was agonizing. I thought all kinds of dire thoughts and had all sorts of "strange symptoms."

Speaking of that phrase "strange symptoms" reminds me of yet another aspect of life after chemo and will probably eventually provoke another in the series of Althea paintings: "Althea Rejects Hypochondriacal Thoughts." Having been a nurse I had little patience with people who constantly think they have some terrible disease when they have a "little cold" or an "upset stomach." Well, again, did I get my "comeuppance " as we say in the Midwest.

Now when I have a stomach ache, I'm convinced I have metastatic cancer throughout the abdomen. If I have slight constipation, I'm terrified I am having a bowel obstruction. If I have a headache, I'm convinced it has gone to my brain. Again, my left brain says these symptoms mean nothing and are ridiculous: they are probably only indicative of a virus or constipation. But because I was caught unexpectedly the first time, I don't want to ignore anything that might signal a return now. I seem to forget that I had no symptoms except spotting before diagnosis so why should any "strange symptoms today" be indicative of Ovarian Cancer returning. It is at those times when I really feel like Althea or like I'm losing it totally.

Then the depression rears its ugly head and I feel a veil of hopelessness descend. I have no control. I'm either going to die, I'm going to have to have more chemo, or I'm simply going to have to go through this agony of waiting for reports for the rest of my life. No one bothered to tell me about these "depression clouds" that descend sometimes without any warning. Perhaps I should have known, but I think I was so elated to finish chemo and still be alive that I didn't think about what would follow. Even after having 4 PET scans with reports of NED, I still fear getting each test result.

Of course the next CA 125 I had, the number went back down to 4 and dropped even lower the summer of 2010 when it was 1. However, I still fret and am consciously trying to get over these fears. I don't know if, or when, that will ever happen but I try to accept that "I'm hanging just like Althea" and I need to live with it. I have a good friend who has kidney dialysis for 3 hours three days of the week, every week and he is not eligible for a transplant because of a heart problem. He is my inspiration. I asked him one time. "Jerry, don't you ever get depressed?" He said "Of course I do." I said "what do you do"? He said "I wait for it to pass." And that is what I'm trying to learn to do – just wait. However, at the same time, I'm trying to learn a lesson from Althea and take myself a little less seriously. She says "Yes I have a potentially life threatening disease, but we are all going to die sometime. I don't have any precious time to waste on 'licking my wounds.' I need to get on with enjoying my life." Can you imagine an Althea painting on this advice?

ALTHEA REACTS TO A GOOD REPORT AND CELEBRATES©

When Althea gets a good CA 125 report she goes "out on the town" and celebrates. As the more aged and "shop worn" half of the duo, I usually have an extra gin and tonic and a steak at home with my husband. As the outrageous fun loving person that Althea is, she has a good time every day despite the precariousness of her situation and that is what I'm trying to learn to do. We can't control the future, the past or even the present. All we can do is enjoy it and trust that "things will all work out" as my mother used to say.

Incidentally, Althea and I get our love of gold and adornments from my mother who, despite being a farm wife who milked the cows, always wore as her milking attire, earrings with a turban, an old man's shirt and jeans. I feel undressed without jewelry (preferably gold) and Althea feels undressed without gold trim on her clothes or feathers on her head.

Because we can't control how long we live, it is important to me how I live. One woman who has been a cancer survivor for 20 years said: "When I was diagnosed with Ovarian Cancer, I vowed I wouldn't do anything I don't want to do and I haven't." And I've tried to take her advice to heart.

I don't mean I live in a dirty shack or eat take out because I both clean and cook. But I try to ask myself whether a chore really needs to be done or whether I just do it from habit since I've always been an A type personality.

The other day I had several things to do after I read the paper. But my 5 month old Bengal Hoffie (who is perfectly named as she is afraid of nothing and models determination and hope for me every day) crawled on my lap and began purring. I decided what the heck and gave myself up to the warmth of her small body and the sound and vibration of her little motor. Before OC, I would have petted her several times and gone about my work.

I also think each of us has to decide what in life renews our spirit and gives us courage and hope. Alternative forms of medicine are great: exercise therapy, good nutrition, meditation, yoga, Chinese medicine, acupuncture, pilates, hobbies like paintings or our pets. What works for one doesn't necessarily work for another; I try to listen to Althea the self-healer who says: " find a way to integrate your physical, mental, emotional, and spiritual selves and help heal yourself."

In other words, see life as beautiful each and every day, something I never realized before, and I'm trying to live totally in the present, not in the past or the future. For example, I've begun wearing my favorite perfume every day, not saving my "best clothes" only for special occasions, and treating myself occasionally to a decadent dark chocolate goodie loaded with nuts and caramel. Why wait to do things? Do them now! – Althea sure would!

Althea tends her Healing Garden wearing outrageous and completely inappropriate clothing just like my mother. However, not only is she nurturing herself in doing this, but she is beautifying the world for others.

Again, Althea has shown me that it is important to heal myself by painting but to paint for something worthwhile – to give something back to the world. As I said earlier, Nicki's Circle provides me with nurturance and comfort. I try to give the same comfort through painting healing gardens, sometimes with Althea's butterfly, for others like me, whether their illness is kidney disease, heart disease, Ovarian Cancer, prostate cancer, breast cancer, or any other disease. Having been really ill for the first time in 67 years, I now know how we all hurt not only physically, but emotionally and psychologically. A part of our self- healing must come from within us. But another part of my own self- healing comes from "what I put out there or make available for others." Painting Althea makes me happy, heals me, and takes my mind off myself; in sharing her, I am trying to do the same for other women with Ovarian Cancer - to illustrate that we can find a balance only if we do not take ourselves too seriously.

One of the most difficult aspects of having Ovarian Cancer is surviving without losing hope. Those of us who constantly research treatments for and clinical trial results on Ovarian Cancer sometimes are excited by new possibilities of treatment, and then we are thrown back into hopelessness as additional reports surface saying the treatments don't work. Focusing on statistics is focusing on what has happened in the past and what, therefore, could be possible hypothetically. However, the statistics on Ovarian Cancer must be negatively impacted by the fact that not all women have access to great gynecological/oncological surgeons and, therefore, don't get the best possible treatment. If we only believe the statistics, we are overlooking the promise of the future.

ALTHEA FOCUSES ON PROMISING FUTURE THERAPIES

    Althea, the forever-resilient-one, chooses to focus on the possibilities that are currently being explored and/or in the pipeline. In this last painting she gazes at several models of pharmaceutical categories emerging from scientific studies today. For example, antiangiogenic biological drugs seem promising because rather than killing cancer cells, they choke off the blood supply that could nurture any remaining cancer cells after chemo. Although they are less harmful to the body than cytoxic agents, antiangiogenic drugs do, have side effects, sometimes, and for some people, the worst of which are bowel perforation, slow healing, bleeding problems or high blood pressure. While biological antiangiogenic drugs seem to be promising, many more trials are needed to determine how to make their effects last longer and make them work on all patients.

    Another promising field of study is the immunological approach to stopping cancer cells from multiplying or creating vaccines which will provoke dendritic cells to develop in such a way that they fight cancer cells. In this approach, scientists take immunoglobulin samples obtained from a woman's tumor and reinject the antigen back into the body – hence provoking the body's T "helper" cells to fight off any remaining tumor cells. Although this therapy is very promising, it also doesn't always work on everyone.

In addition, researchers today are manipulating DNA repair drugs and are developing substances that will block the action of proteins in the DNA if their action is such that they allow cancer cells to multiply. Poly(ADP-ribose) polymerase – 1 or PARP inhibitors are promising target drugs in particular for patients who are BRCA1 and BRCA 2 positive. However, a need also exists for clinical trials investigating PARP's effects on sporadic Ovarian Cancer as well. Yet years of clinical trials will be necessary before these drugs become available to most Ovarian Cancer patients.

Research and development of many other new cancer drugs and approval via clinical trials and the FDA remain essential if we are ever to have a cure for Ovarian Cancer or any other cancer. Yet in the tough economic times of 2010, venture capital money for trials and marketing is disappearing. Also we don't know what the effects of the health care reform will be on research. While many ideas are hatched in academe, money used to develop them comes from both the government and pharmaceutical companies. Also if the criteria for success in a clinical trial for a drug is overall survival results, and not progression free survival, patients who have chronic diseases like Ovarian Cancer will suffer.

While Althea looks into each of these general categories of pharmaceutical development and tries to do her part in helping herself stay physically and emotionally alive until a cure is found, she has to balance her hope against the reality of slowness and low funding. That balance is definitely not an easy state to achieve.

When a doctor like mine, who always has between 6 or 8 clinical trials going, says my job is to keep you alive for the next 10 years (perhaps having to try chemo regime after chemo regime) and after that there will be a cure, you know she is hopeful. And while we can help ourselves by eating properly, staying strong by exercising, and keeping our immune system intact, we have to balance all those physical actions against keeping our minds emotionally hopeful.

CONCLUSION

Alone, I often feel overwhelmed and doomed by the reach of this awful disease, Ovarian Cancer, into both my body and mind. I think I must be abnormal. Then, as I talk with others, I realize we all go through the same doubts and emotional swings. Some days we are happy and other days we crash. But I now realize these swings, humorously enacted on the canvas by Althea, are entirely normal given what we have to cope with in keeping our balance between hope and enjoyment of life and our fears and doubts.

Althea and her series help me keep the good and bad in perspective. She may be gaudy, campy, outrageous and downright trashy at times, but she makes me laugh. The cliché "laughter is good for the soul" is so true. It releases hormone which are good for our bodies as well as our minds.

So Althea and I hope that in sharing with you our teetering- journey through the ovarian-cancer-circus of our lives, you will recognize that we all go through so many of the same experiences. We are all survivors from the day of our diagnosis until the end of our lives. But the quality of that survivorship is up to us – to the Althea, the self healer in each of us. So I say to myself and to all of you what Althea would say: "You go girl!"

Annette Bennington McElhiney is a former RN as well as a B.A., M.A., and Ph.D in English and American literature. She is an Emeritus Professor (retired) of English and Women's Studies at Metropolitan State College in Denver, CO. She was diagnosed with Ovarian Cancer III C in 07/08 and continues her battle against the disease. Being aware of plentiful informational material on the medical and physical aspects of Ovarian Cancer, she felt a need existed for material preparing one for the emotional roller coaster that such a diagnosis brings in its wake. As a largely self taught amateur painter and former academic writer, she chose to combine the two in this humorous portrayal of feisty Althea, the self-healer, who tackles balancing her hope of controlling the disease against her fears of reoccurrence as she follows the typical follow-up care of an Ovarian Cancer Patient.

All the proceeds from this and other booklets as well as any paintings will go to Ovarian Cancer Research. Her paintings are available on her web page by googling Annette McElhiney at Fine Arts of America. She can be reached at annettemcelhiney@comcast.net.

Made in the USA
Charleston, SC
06 May 2014